# ESSENTIAL ELEMENTS®
# POP SONGS
## FOR KEYBOARD PERCUSSION

ISBN 978-1-70515-031-3

World headquarters, contact:
**Hal Leonard**
7777 West Bluemound Road
Milwaukee, WI 53213
Email: info@halleonard.com

In Europe, contact:
**Hal Leonard Europe Limited**
1 Red Place
London, W1K 6PL
Email: info@halleonardeurope.com

In Australia, contact:
**Hal Leonard Australia Pty. Ltd.**
4 Lentara Court
Cheltenham, Victoria, 3192 Australia
Email: info@halleonard.com.au

# THE MEDALLION CALLS

## from PIRATES OF THE CARIBBEAN: THE CURSE OF THE BLACK PEARL

Music by KLAUS BADELT

# GAME OF THRONES

## Theme from the HBO Series GAME OF THRONES

By RAMIN DJAWADI

# THE RAINBOW CONNECTION
## from THE MUPPET MOVIE

Words and Music by
PAUL WILLIAMS and KENNETH L. ASCHER

Moderately, with a lilt

# THE AVENGERS
## from THE AVENGERS

Composed by ALAN SILVESTRI

Moderately, with intensity

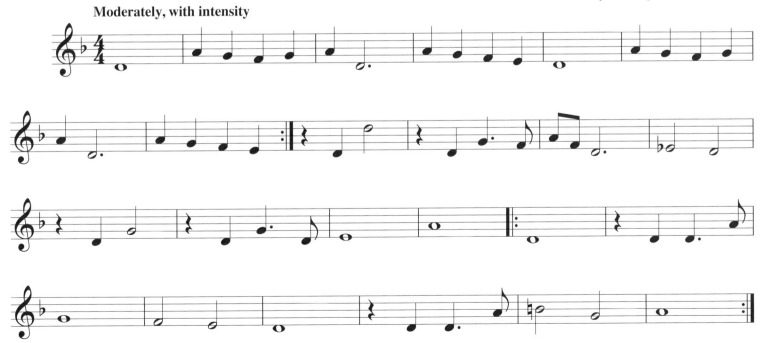

# HALLELUJAH

Words and Music by LEONARD COHEN

# KERNKRAFT 400

By EMANUEL GUENTHER and FLORIAN SENFTER

# HAPPY

Words and Music by PHARRELL WILLIAMS

**Moderately Fast**

# SKYFALL

### from the Motion Picture SKYFALL

Words and Music by
ADELE ADKINS and PAUL EPWORTH

**Moderately Slow, Mysterious**

# HAVANA

**Words and Music by CAMILA CABELLO, LOUIS BELL, PHARRELL WILLIAMS, ADAM FEENEY, ALI TAMPOSI, JEFFERY LAMAR WILLIAMS, BRIAN LEE, ANDREW WOTMAN, BRITTANY HAZZARD and KAAN GUNESBERK**

Moderately, with a Latin Groove

# HIGH HOPES

**Words and Music by BRENDON URIE, WILLIAM LOBBAN BEAN, JONAS JEBERG, SAMUEL HOLLANDER, JACOB SINCLAIR, JENNY OWEN YOUNGS, ILSEY JUBER, LAUREN PRITCHARD and TAYLA PARX**

Moderately

# SEÑORITA

**Words and Music by CAMILA CABELLO,
CHARLOTTE AITCHISON, JACK PATTERSON,
SHAWN MENDES, MAGNUS HOIBERG,
BENJAMIN LEVIN, ALI TAMPOSI
and ANDREW WOTMAN**

Moderate Latin Groove

# SEVEN NATION ARMY

**Words and Music by JACK WHITE**

Moderate Rock

# HEAVEN

Words and Music by SHY CARTER,
LINDSAY RIMES and MATTHEW MCGINN

**Slow Rock**

# DYNAMITE

Words and Music by
JESSICA AGOMBAR and DAVID STEWART

**Moderately Fast**

# COUNTING STARS

Words and Music by RYAN TEDDER

**Moderately**

# SUCKER

Words and Music by NICK JONAS, JOSEPH JONAS,
MILES ALE, MUSTAFA AHMED, RYAN TEDDER, LOUIS BELL,
ADAM FEENEY, KEVIN JONAS and HOMER STEINWEISS

**Pop Rock**

# LET IT GO
## from FROZEN

Music and Lyrics by
KRISTEN ANDERSON-LOPEZ and ROBERT LOPEZ

**Half-Time Feel, Mysterious**

# WILDEST DREAMS

Words and Music by TAYLOR SWIFT,
MAX MARTIN and SHELLBACK

**Moderately Fast**

# I GOTTA FEELING

Words and Music by WILL ADAMS,
ALLAN PINEDA, JAIME GOMEZ, STACY FERGUSON,
DAVID GUETTA and FREDERIC RIESTERER

**Moderately Fast**

# VIDA LA VIDA

Words and Music by
GUY BERRYMAN, JON BUCKLAND
WILL CHAMPION and CHRIS MARTIN

**With Intensity**

# THIS IS ME
## from THE GREATEST SHOWMAN

Words and Music by
BENJ PASEK and JUSTIN PAUL

**With Emotion**

# WE ARE THE CHAMPIONS

Words and Music by
FREDDIE MERCURY

**Moderately Slow**

# BLINDING LIGHTS

Words and Music by ABEL TESFAYE,
MAX MARTIN, JASON QUENNEVILLE,
OSCAR HOLTER and AHMAD BALSHE

**Fast, Driving Retro Pop**

# DON'T STOP BELIEVIN'

Words and Music by STEVE PERRY,
NEAL SCHON and JONATHAN CAIN

**Moderate Rock**

# NO TIME TO DIE
## from NO TIME TO DIE

Words and Music by BILLIE EILISH O'CONNELL
and FINNEAS O'CONNELL

# LEAD THE WAY
## from RAYA AND THE LAST DRAGON

Music and Lyrics by JHENE AIKO

# YOU WILL BE FOUND
## from DEAR EVAN HANSEN

Music and Lyrics by
BENJ PASEK and JUSTIN PAUL

**Reverent**

# THE IMPERIAL MARCH (Darth Vader's Theme)
## from STAR WARS: THE EMPIRE STRIKES BACK

Music by JOHN WILLIAMS

**March**

# BELIEVER

**Words and Music by DAN REYNOLDS, WAYNE SERMON, BEN MCKEE, DANIEL PLATZMAN, JUSTIN TRANTOR, MATTIAS LARSSON and ROBIN FREDRICKSSON**

**Rock Shuffle!**

# ANGRY BIRDS THEME

**By ARI PULKKINEN**

**Ooom-pah Style**